WHISKY

CLASSIC &
CONTEMPORARY
COCKTAILS

An Hachette UK Company
www.hachette.co.uk

First published in Great Britain in 2018 by Hamlyn,
an imprint of Octopus Publishing Group Ltd
Carmelite House, 50 Victoria Embankment, London EC4Y 0DZ
www.octopusbooks.co.uk

ISBN 978-0-75373-331-8

A CIP catalogue record for this book is available from the British Library

Printed and bound in China

10 9 8 7 6 5 4 3 2 1

Publisher: Lucy Pessell
Designer: Lisa Layton
Editor: Sarah Vaughan
Production Manager: Caroline Alberti
Cover and interior motifs created by: Abhimanyu Bose, LSE Designs, Magicon,
Valeriy, Wuppdidu, Waiyi Fung. All from *The Noun Project*.

The measure that has been used in the recipes is based on a bar jigger, which is 25 ml (1 fl oz).
If preferred, a different volume can be used, providing the proportions are kept constant within a
drink and suitable adjustments are made to spoon measurements, where they occur.

Standard level spoon measurements are used in all recipes.
1 tablespoon = one 15 ml spoon
1 teaspoon = one 5 ml spoon

This book contains cocktails made with raw or lightly cooked eggs. It is prudent for more vulnerable
people to avoid uncooked or lightly cooked cocktails made with eggs.

Some of this material previously appeared in *Hamlyn All Colour Cookery: 200 Classic Cocktails* and
501 Must-Drink Cocktails.

WHISKY

CLASSIC &
CONTEMPORARY
COCKTAILS

hamlyn

CONTENTS

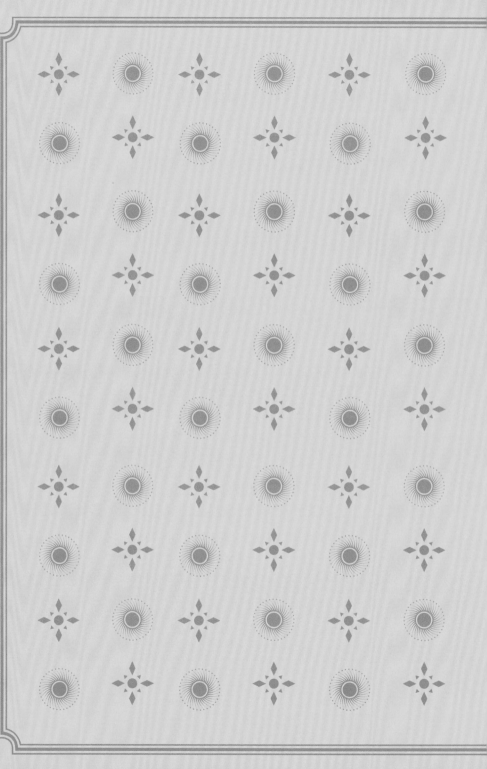

A BRIEF HISTORY OF WHISKY & COCKTAILS

The origin of the word 'COCKTAIL' is widely disputed.

Initially used to describe the docked tails of horses that were not thoroughbred (which hasn't much to do with a Singapore Sling), the alleged first definition of a 'cocktail' appeared in New York's *The Balance and Columbian Repository*. In response to the question 'What is a cocktail?' the editor replied: 'it is a stimulating liquor, composed of spirits of any kind, sugar, water and bitters... in as much as it renders the heart stout and bold, at the same time that it fuddles the head... because a person, having swallowed a glass of it, is ready to swallow anything else.' Which sounds a little more like it.

However it began, this delightful act of mixing varying amounts of spirits, sugar and bitters has evolved, after decades of fine crafting, experimentation and even 13 years of prohibition in the United States, into the 'cocktail' we know and love. Each one a masterpiece. Each one to be made just right for you.

In the century since Harry Craddock concocted the Corpse Reviver and the White Lady, James Bond has insisted on breaking the number 1 rule to not shake a Martini every time he goes to the bar, and *Sex and the City* has introduced a whole new generation of drinkers to the very pink, very fabulous, Cosmopolitan cocktail. And the idea it can be paired with a burger and fries. Which is fine by us.

Go forth and make yours a Martini. Or a French Afternoon at gin o'clock on a mizzly Monday morning.

WHISKY, or **WHISKEY**, is a caramel to deep brown spirit made from fermented grains such as rye and barley, and is aged in wooden barrels.

Whisky is as old as the hills. Probably the hills of Ireland but we can't be quite sure so we'll stick with 'hills'.

'Whisky' is an anglicization of the Gaelic 'water of life', from the Latin 'aqua vitae'. Had the people in charge of translation back then known it by its other name, 'fire water', perhaps we'd now call it Frisky. We digress.

'Whisky' or 'whiskey' is a common spelling conundrum but the correct name is simply determined by where it was made. As a general rule, 'whisky' is made in Scotland, Canada and the rest of the world, while Ireland and America use 'whiskey'. And where whisk(e)y comes from is of great importance to a lot of people in a lot of places.

From America's smooth, corn mash bourbons and rye-y ryes, to Ireland's triple-distilled blends and Scotland's famed single malts (and every combination and exception in between), Whisky is a whole w(h)ide w(h)orld of w(h)ater - life or fire - to discover.

Here's a collection of recipes that'll help you do just that.

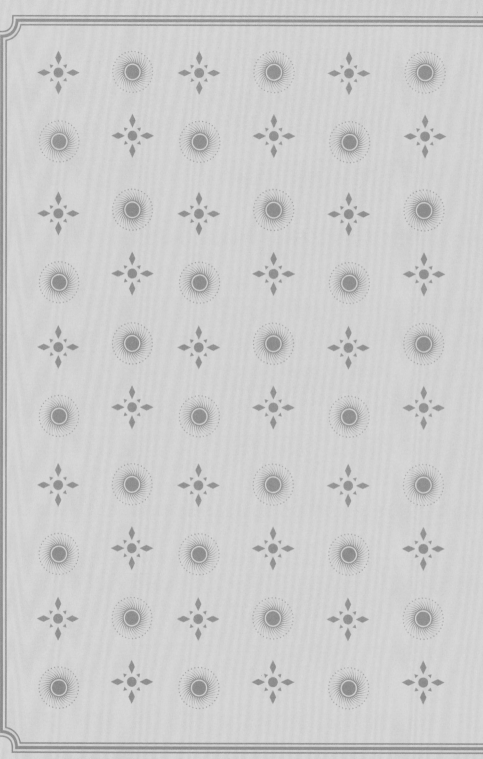

LIGHT & FLORAL

STONE FENCE

1 CRISP APPLE, PLUS AN APPLE SLICE, TO GARNISH

2 MEASURES RYE WHISKEY

1 MEASURE SODA WATER

Juice the apple and pour into a glass full of ice cubes.

Add the whiskey and soda water and garnish with an apple slice.

ICHI HIGHBALL

1½ MEASURES SCOTCH WHISKY

1 MEASURE UMESHU

SODA WATER, TO TOP

4 CUCUMBER SLICES, PLUS EXTRA STRIPS,

TO GARNISH

Add 4 cucumber slices, 1 measure umeshu and 1½ measures Scotch whisky to a glass and press the cucumber with the end of a bar spoon to release some of the flavour.

Fill a collins glass with ice cubes, top with 4 measures soda water and stir.

Garnish with a cucumber strip.

MINT JULEP II

1 MEASURE BOURBON

½ TBSP CASTER SUGAR

1 TBSP SODA WATER

3 SPRIGS MINT, PLUS EXTRA, TO GARNISH

Crush the mint with the sugar in an old-fashioned glass or large tumbler and rub it around the insides of the glass. Discard the mint.

Dissolve the sugar in the soda water, add 3–4 ice cubes and pour the bourbon over it. Do not stir.

Garnish with the extra mint sprig.

15

BENEDICT

3 MEASURES SCOTCH WHISKY

1 MEASURE BÉNÉDICTINE

DRY GINGER ALE, TO TOP

LEMON, TO GARNISH

Put 3–4 ice cubes into a mixing glass and pour the Bénédictine and whisky over it.

Stir evenly without splashing and then pour without straining into a chilled highball glass.

Top up with ginger ale and garnish with a lemon wedge.

17

ITALIAN HEATHER

4 MEASURES SCOTCH WHISKY

1 MEASURE GALLIANO

LEMON, TO GARNISH

Put the ice cubes into a tall glass
and stir in the whisky and Galliano.

Garnish with a lemon rind twist.

CHAMPAGNE JULEP

1 MEASURE COGNAC

1 TSP SUGAR

8 MINT LEAVES

CHAMPAGNE, TO TOP

MINT SPRIGS, TO GARNISH

Add the Cognac, sugar and mint leaves to a highball glass filled with crushed ice and churn.

Top with Champagne and more crushed ice and garnish with mint sprigs.

19

VIRGINIA MINT JULEP

3 MEASURES BOURBON

1 TSP SUGAR SYRUP

9 YOUNG MINT SPRIGS, PLUS EXTRA, TO GARNISH

Muddle the mint and sugar syrup in an iced silver mug or tall glass.

Fill the mug or glass with crushed ice, pour the bourbon over the ice and stir gently.

Pack in more crushed ice and stir until a frost forms.

Wrap the mug or glass in a table napkin and garnish with a mint sprig.

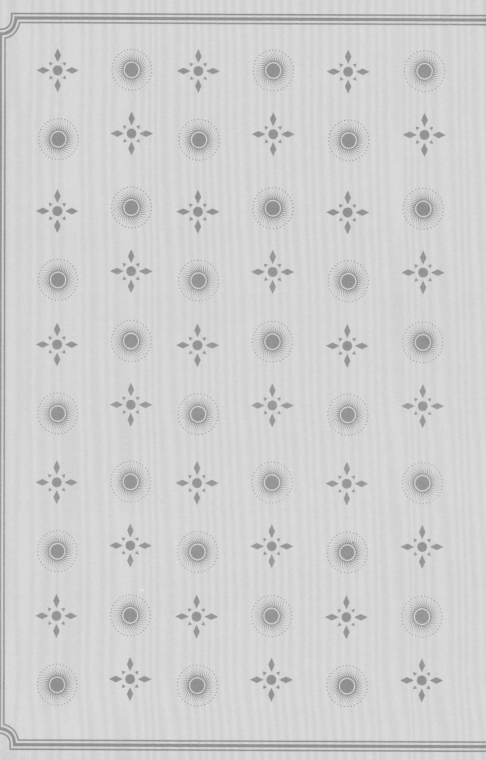

VIBRANT & ZESTY

BOURBON MULE

2 MEASURES BOURBON

3 TSP ORANGE LIQUEUR

4 MEASURES GINGER BEER

2 DASHES ANGOSTURA BITTERS

2 TSP LEMON JUICE

LEMON & LIME, TO GARNISH

Fill a glass with ice cubes, add the remaining ingredients and stir.

Garnish with a lemon and a lime wedge.

CHUCK BUCK MULE

2 ORANGE & CHERRY-INFUSED BOURBON

(SEE PAGE 115)

4 TSP TRIPLE SEC

2 TSP LEMON JUICE

2 TSP GINGER JUICE

MARASCHINO CHERRY OR ORANGE, TO GARNISH

Fill a collins glass with ice cubes, add all the ingredients except the soda water and stir.

Top up with 4 measures soda water and garnish with a maraschino cherry or orange slice.

HIGHLAND HIGHBALL

2 MEASURES SCOTCH WHISKY

3 TSP CITRUS OLEO-SACCHARUM

2 TSP GINGER JUICE

2 TSP LEMON JUICE

2 DASHES ANGOSTURA BITTERS

SODA WATER, TO TOP

LEMON & CRYSTALLIZED GINGER, TO

GARNISH

Add all the ingredients except the soda water to a cocktail shaker and fill with ice.

Strain into a collins glass filled with ice cubes, then top up with 4 measures soda water.

Garnish with lemon wedge and crystallized ginger.

27

SCOTCH GINGER HIGHBALL

2 MEASURES SCOTCH WHISKY

1 MEASURE LEMON JUICE

3 TSP SUGAR SYRUP

4 MEASURES GINGER ALE

FRESH ROOT GINGER, TO GARNISH

Pour the whisky, lemon juice, sugar syrup and ginger ale into a glass filled with ice cubes and stir.

Garnish with a slice of fresh root ginger.

STONE STAIRS

1½ MEASURES SCOTCH WHISKY

2 TSP BÉNÉDICTINE

JUICE OF ½ GRANNY SMITH APPLE

JUICE OF ½ PEAR

1 MEASURE SODA WATER

PEAR, TO GARNISH

Juice ½ Granny Smith apple and ½ pear.

Pour the juice into an old-fashioned glass full of ice cubes, add 1½ measures Scotch whisky, 2 teaspoons Bénédictine and 1 measure soda water.

Garnish with a pear slice and serve.

SPICED PEAR COCKTAIL

1½ MEASURES BOURBON

2 TSP BÉNÉDICTINE

2 TSP NUTMEG SYRUP

2 TSP LEMON JUICE

10 REDCURRANTS

½ RIPE PEAR, PLUS EXTRA, TO GARNISH

Add ½ ripe pear, cut into chunks, and 10 redcurrants to a cocktail shaker and muddle.

Add the remaining ingredients and shake.

Strain into an old-fashioned glass full of ice cubes and garnish with pear slices.

WILLIAM'S PEAR

2 MEASURES BOURBON

4 TSP LEMON JUICE

½ RIPE PEAR CUT INTO CHUNKS,

PLUS EXTRA SLICES, TO GARNISH

3 TSP REDCURRANT JAM

2 TSP SUGAR SYRUP

Add the pear and jam to a cocktail shaker and muddle.

Add the remaining ingredients and shake and strain into a glass full of ice cubes

Garnish with pear slices.

CAPRICORN

1 MEASURE BOURBON

½ MEASURE APRICOT BRANDY

½ MEASURE LEMON JUICE

2 MEASURES ORANGE JUICE

ORANGE, TO GARNISH

Put 2–3 cracked ice cubes into a cocktail shaker and add the bourbon, apricot brandy and fruit juices.

Shake to mix.

Strain into an old-fashioned glass over the a few more cracked ice cubes.

Garnish with an orange slice.

TAR

3 MEASURES SCOTCH WHISKY

½ TSP GRENADINE

1 MEASURE CRÈME DE CACAO

JUICE OF 1 LEMON

Pour in the lemon juice, grenadine, crème de cacao and whisky into a cocktail shaker and a few ice cubes.

Shake until a frost forms and strain into a chilled cocktail glass.

Serve with a straw.

35

PEACH
SMASH

4 MEASURES BOURBON

12 MINT LEAVES, PLUS SPRIGS, TO GARNISH

6 PEACH SLICES

4 TSP CASTER SUGAR

6 LEMON SLICES, PLUS EXTRA, TO GARNISH

Muddle the mint leaves, peach and lemon slices and sugar in a cocktail shaker.

Add the bourbon and some ice cubes and shake well.

Strain over cracked ice into 2 glasses and garnish each with a mint sprig and a lemon slice.

RHETT BUTLER

4 MEASURES BOURBON

8 MEASURES CRANBERRY JUICE

2 TBSP LIME JUICE

4 TBSP SUGAR SYRUP

Half-fill a cocktail shaker with ice cubes, add all the ingredients and shake well.

Strain into 2 old-fashioned glasses filled with ice.

GOLDEN DAISY

3 MEASURES SCOTCH WHISKY

½ MEASURE COINTREAU

JUICE OF 1 LEMON

1 TSP SUGAR SYRUP

LIME, TO GARNISH

Put 4–5 ice cubes into a cocktail shaker and pour the whisky, Cointreau, lemon juice and sugar syrup over it.

Shake until a frost forms and strain into an old-fashioned glass.

Garnish with a lime wedge.

39

BOURBON FIXED

2 MEASURES BOURBON

1 MEASURE MORELLO CHERRY PURÉE

1 TBSP LEMON JUICE

2 TSP SUGAR SYRUP

LIME & CHERRIES, TO GARNISH

Put some ice cubes into a cocktail shaker with the bourbon, cherry purée, lemon juice and sugar syrup and shake to mix.

Strain into an old-fashioned glass filled with ice cubes and garnish with lemon rind spirals and 2 cherries on a cocktail stick.

LEPRECHAUN DANCER

1 MEASURE IRISH WHISKEY

1 MEASURE LEMON JUICE

SODA WATER, TO TOP

DRY GINGER ALE, TO TOP

LEMON, TO GARNISH

Combine 4–5 ice cubes, whiskey and lemon juice in a highball glass.

Top up with equal measures of soda water and ginger ale and garnish with a lemon rind twist.

CANADIAN DAISY

2 MEASURES CANADIAN WHISKY

1 TSP BRANDY

2 TSP LEMON JUICE

1 TSP RASPBERRY JUICE

1 TSP SUGAR SYRUP

SODA WATER, TO TOP

RASPBERRIES, TO GARNISH

Put some ice cubes into a cocktail shaker with the whisky, fruit juices and sugar syrup and shake well before straining into a tall glass.

Add a few ice cubes and top up with soda water.

Garnish with raspberries and float the brandy on top of the drink.

43

NERIDA

3 MEASURES SCOTCH WHISKY

JUICE OF ½ LIME OR LEMON

DRY GINGER ALE, TO TOP

LIME OR LEMON, TO GARNISH

Put a handful of ice cubes, the lime or lemon juice and the whisky into a cocktail shaker and shake until a frost forms.

Pour without straining into a chilled collins glass.

Top up with ginger ale, stir gently and garnish with lime or lemon slices.

44

MIKE
COLLINS

3 MEASURES IRISH WHISKEY

JUICE OF 1 LEMON

1 TBSP SUGAR SYRUP

SODA WATER, TO TOP

ORANGE & COCKTAIL CHERRY, TO GARNISH

Put 5–6 ice cubes into a cocktails shaker and pour in the lemon juice, sugar syrup and whiskey and shake until a frost forms.

Pour without straining into a tumbler or collins glass and add an orange slice and a cocktail cherry on a stick.

45

Top up with soda water, stir lightly and serve, garnished with an orange rind spiral.

ECLIPSE

2 MEASURES JACK DANIEL'S WHISKEY

½ MEASURE CHAMBORD

½ MEASURE LIME JUICE

1 MEASURE CRANBERRY JUICE

1 MEASURE RASPBERRY JUICE

1 DASH SUGAR SYRUP

RASPBERRY & LIME, TO GARNISH

Put some ice cubes into a cocktail shaker with all the other ingredients and shake well.

Strain into a large highball glass filled with crushed ice.

Garnish with a raspberry and a lime wedge and serve with long straws.

ROAMIN' THE GLOAMIN'

2 MEASURES SCOTCH WHISKY

1 MEASURE COINTREAU

2 TBSP ORANGE JUICE

ORANGE, TO GARNISH

Put a handful of ice cubes into a cocktail shaker.

Add the whisky, Cointreau and orange juice and shake until a frost forms.

Pour into an old-fashioned glass and garnish with an orange slice.

BLINKER

½ MEASURE CANADIAN WHISKY

¾ MEASURE GRAPEFRUIT JUICE

¼ MEASURE GRENADINE

ORANGE, TO GARNISH

Put some cracked ice into a cocktail shaker with the whisky, grapefruit juice and grenadine and shake well.

Serve in a chilled cocktail glass and garnish with an orange rind twist.

LYNCHBURG LEMONADE

1½ MEASURES JACK DANIEL'S WHISKEY

1 MEASURE COINTREAU

1 MEASURE LEMON JUICE

LEMONADE, TO TOP

LEMON, TO GARNISH

Put some ice cubes into a cocktail shaker with the Jack Daniel's, Cointreau and lemon juice and shake well.

Strain into a glass filled with ice cubes and top up with lemonade.

Stir and garnish with lemon slices.

NEW YORKER

1 MEASURE SCOTCH WHISKY

1 TSP LIME JUICE

1 TSP ICING SUGAR

FINELY GRATED RIND OF ½ LEMON

LEMON, TO GARNISH

Put a few cracked ice cubes into a cocktail shaker and add the whisky, lime juice and sugar.

Shake until a frost forms and strain into an old-fashioned glass.

Sprinkle the grated lemon rind over the surface and garnish the rim of the glass with a lemon rind spiral.

CLIQUET

3 MEASURES BOURBON OR SCOTCH WHISKY

1 TBSP DARK RUM

JUICE OF 1 ORANGE

ORANGE, TO GARNISH

Put a handful of ice cubes into a mixing glass and pour the orange juice, bourbon or whisky and rum over the ice.

Stir vigorously, then strain into a sour glass.

Garnish with an orange rind twist.

53

GODFATHER SOUR

1½ MEASURES BOURBON

1 MEASURE AMARETTO DI SARONNO LIQUEUR

1 MEASURE LEMON JUICE

1 TSP SUGAR SYRUP

LEMON, TO GARNISH

Put some ice cubes into a cocktail shaker with the bourbon, Amaretto di Saronno, lemon juice and sugar syrup and shake well.

Strain into a small old-fashioned glass filled with ice cubes and garnish with lemon slices.

BOURBON SLOE GIN

1½ MEASURES BOURBON

½ MEASURE SLOE GIN

½ MEASURE LEMON JUICE

1 TBSP SUGAR SYRUP

LEMON & PEACH, TO GARNISH

Put some ice cubes into a cocktail shaker with the bourbon, sloe gin, lemon juice and sugar syrup and shake well.

Strain into a cocktail glass over crushed ice.

Garnish with lemon and peach slices.

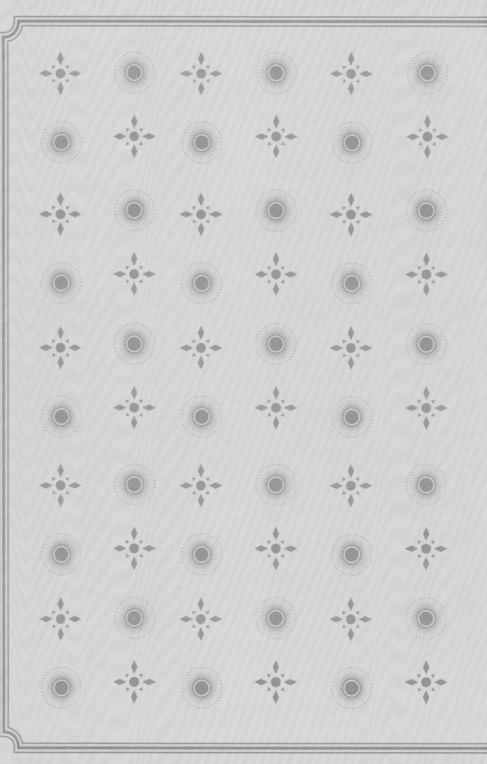

INTENSE
& SULTRY

WHISKY HIGHBALL

2 MEASURES SCOTCH WHISKY

1 DASH ANGOSTURA BITTERS

4 MEASURES SODA WATER

LEMON, TO GARNISH

Add 3 large ice cubes, the whisky and Angostura bitters to a glass.

Stir gently, then fill the glass with more ice cubes and top up with the soda water.

Garnish with a lemon twist.

BIG BUFF

2 MEASURES BUFFALO TRACE BOURBON

2 TSP CHAMBORD

1 DASH LIME JUICE

3 MEASURES CRANBERRY JUICE

1 STRAWBERRY, HULLED

3 RASPBERRIES

3 BLUEBERRIES, PLUS EXTRA, TO GARNISH

Muddle the berries and Chambord in a cocktail shaker.

Add the bourbon, lime juice, cranberry juice and a few ice cubes.

Shake, then pour without straining into a highball glass and garnish with blueberries.

WHIZZ BANG

3 MEASURES SCOTCH WHISKY

½ TSP GRENADINE

1 MEASURE DRY VERMOUTH

1 DROP PERNOD

3 DROPS ORANGE BITTERS

Put 4–5 ice cubes into a mixing glass, shake the bitters over the it and pour in the grenadine, vermouth and whisky.

Stir vigorously, then strain into a chilled cocktail glass.

Add the Pernod and stir again.

EARLY NIGHT

1 MEASURE SCOTCH WHISKY

1 MEASURE GINGER WINE

1 TBSP LEMON JUICE

1 MEASURE CLEAR HONEY

2 MEASURES HOT WATER

LEMON, TO GARNISH

Put the lemon juice and honey into a toddy glass and stir well.

Add the whisky and continue stirring.

Stir in the hot water, then add the ginger wine.

Garnish with a lemon slice and stir continuously while drinking it hot.

BLACK JACK

¾ MEASURE JACK DANIEL'S

¾ MEASURE BLACK SAMBUCA

Pour the Jack Daniel's into a
shot glass.

Using the back of a bar spoon,
slowly float the sambuca over
the Jack Daniel's.

GINGER FIX

1 MEASURE BLENDED SCOTCH WHISKY

1 MEASURE GINGER WINE

2 DASHES ANGOSTURA BITTERS

4 MEASURES SODA WATER

LEMON, TO GARNISH

Fill the glass with ice cubes,
add the remaining ingredients
and stir.

Garnish with a lemon wedge.

65

BOBBY BURNS

1 MEASURE SCOTCH WHISKY

1 MEASURE DRY VERMOUTH

1 TBSP BÉNÉDICTINE

LEMON, TO GARNISH

Put some ice cubes into a cocktail shaker with the whisky, vermouth and Bénédictine and shake until a frost forms.

Strain into a chilled cocktail glass and garnish with a lemon rind strip.

66

ST CLEMENT'S MANHATTAN

1 MEASURE ORANGE-INFUSED BOURBON

(SEE PAGE 115)

1 MEASURE LEMON-INFUSED BOURBON

(SEE PAGE 115)

1 TBSP SWEET VERMOUTH

4 DASHES ANGOSTURA BITTERS

ORANGE & LEMON, TO GARNISH

Put some ice cubes into a mixing glass with the whiskies, vermouth and bitters and stir well.

Strain into a chilled cocktail glass and garnish with orange and lemon rind twists.

67

ZOOM

2 MEASURES SCOTCH WHISKY

1 TSP CLEAR HONEY

1 MEASURE CHILLED WATER

1 MEASURE SINGLE CREAM

Put some ice cubes into a cocktail shaker, add the whisky, honey, chilled water and cream and shake well.

Strain into an old-fashioned glass.

SILKY PIN

1 MEASURE SCOTCH WHISKY

1 MEASURE DRAMBUIE CREAM LIQUEUR

Fill an old-fashioned glass
with ice cubes and pour the
whisky and Drambuie Cream
Liqueur over them.

Stir gently.

ROLLIN' STONED

2 MEASURES THAI WHISKY

1 DASH BANANA LIQUEUR

1 DASH RASPBERRY LIQUEUR

1 DASH LIME JUICE

2 MEASURES ORANGE JUICE

2 MEASURES PINEAPPLE JUICE

ORANGES & COCKTAIL CHERRIES, TO GARNISH

Put all the ingredients into a cocktail shaker and shake and strain into a highball glass filled with ice cubes.

Garnish with orange slices and cocktail cherries on a cocktail stick.

Serve with long straws.

AMERICAN BELLE

½ MEASURE BOURBON

½ MEASURE CHERRY LIQUEUR

½ MEASURE AMARETTO DI SARONNO LIQUEUR

Pour the cherry liqueur into a shot glass and, using the back of a bar spoon, slowly float the Amaretto di Saronno over the it.

Float the bourbon over the Amaretto in the same way.

CLUB

1 MEASURE SCOTCH WHISKY

2 DASHES ANGOSTURA BITTERS

1 DASH GRENADINE

LEMON & COCKTAIL CHERRY, TO GARNISH

Put some cracked ice into a mixing glass.

Add the bitters, whisky and grenadine and stir well.

Strain into a cocktail glass and garnish with a lemon rind spiral and a cocktail cherry.

ABERDEEN ANGUS

2 MEASURES SCOTCH WHISKY

1 MEASURE DRAMBUIE

1 TSP CLEAR HONEY

2 TSP LIME JUICE

Combine the whisky and honey in a mug and stir until smooth. Add the lime juice.

Warm the Drambuie in a small saucepan over a low heat.

Pour into a ladle, ignite and pour into the mug.

Stir and serve immediately.

SUBURBAN

3 MEASURES BOURBON OR SCOTCH WHISKY

1 MEASURE PORT

1 MEASURE DARK RUM

3 DROPS ORANGE OR ANGOSTURA BITTERS

Put 4–5 ice cubes into a mixing glass, shake the bitters over the them and then pour in the bourbon or whisky, port and rum.

Stir vigorously, then strain into a chilled cocktail glass.

75

BOOMERANG

½ MEASURE JÄGERMEISTER

½ MEASURE BOURBON

Pour the Jägermeister into a shot glass.

Using the back of a bar spoon, slowly float the bourbon over the Jägermeister.

RITZ OLD FASHIONED

1½ MEASURES BOURBON

½ MEASURE GRAND MARNIER

1 DASH LEMON JUICE, PLUS EXTRA,
TO FROST THE GLASS

1 DASH ANGOSTURA BITTERS

CASTER SUGAR

ORANGE OR LEMON, TO GARNISH

Frost the rim of a cocktail glass by
dipping it into lemon juice, then
pressing it into the sugar.

Put a few crushed ice cubes into
a cocktail shaker and add the
remaining ingredients.

Shake to mix, strain into the
prepared glass and garnish with
an orange or lemon rind spiral.

HARLEQUIN

2 MEASURES CANADIAN CLUB WHISKY

½ MEASURE SWEET VERMOUTH

6 DASHES ORANGE BITTERS

5 WHITE GRAPES, PLUS EXTRA, TO GARNISH

Muddle the grapes, vermouth and bitters in an old-fashioned glass.

Half-fill the glass with crushed ice and stir well.

Add the whisky and top up with crushed ice.

Garnish with 2 white grapes.

79

CASSIS

1 MEASURE BOURBON

½ MEASURE DRY VERMOUTH

1 TSP CRÈME DE CASSIS

2 BLUEBERRIES, TO GARNISH

Put some ice cubes into a cocktail shaker and pour in the bourbon, vermouth and crème de cassis.

Shake well, then strain into a chilled cocktail glass and garnish with blueberries on a cocktail stick.

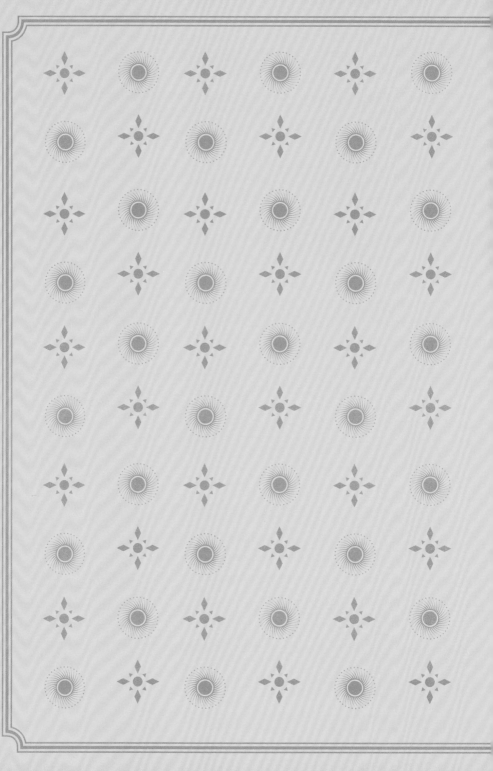

SHARERS &
PUNCHES

MULLED ORCHARD

4 MEASURES BOURBON

6 MEASURES CIDER

4 MEASURES APPLE JUICE

1 MEASURE LEMON JUICE

1 MEASURE SPICED

1 KNOB BUTTER

CINNAMON STICKS, TO GARNISH

Melt the butter in a saucepan over a
gentle heat and add the apple juice,
lemon juice, spiced sugar syrup,
bourbon and cider. Stir until hot.

Pour carefully into a teapot and serve
in heatproof glasses, garnished with
cinnamon sticks.

SOUTHERN BELLE

6 MEASURES BOURBON

200 ML CIDER

2 MEASURES LEMON JUICE

2 MEASURES APPLE JUICE

4 MEASURES YELLOW TEA

2 MEASURES SUGAR SYRUP

APPLE & LEMON, TO GARNISH

Fill a large jug with ice cubes, add 6 measures bourbon, 2 measures lemon juice, 2 measures sugar syrup, 4 measures yellow tea, 2 measures apple juice and 200 ml cider and stir.

Garnish with apple and lemon slices.

BATON BLANC

2 MEASURES BOURBON

200 ML WHEAT BEER

2 MEASURES LEMON JUICE

2 MEASURES ORANGE JUICE

2 MEASURES SUGAR SYRUP

2 TSP MARMALADE

ORANGE, TO GARNISH

Put 4 measures bourbon, 2 measures lemon juice, 2 measures orange juice, 2 measures sugar syrup and 2 teaspoons marmalade in a food processor or blender and blend until smooth.

Pour into a large jug, add 200 ml wheat beer and top up the jug with ice cubes.

Garnish with orange wheels to serve.

BLUE GRASS PUNCH

4 MEASURES BOURBON

3 TSP MARMALADE

2 MEASURES LEMON JUICE

1 MEASURE SUGAR SYRUP

2 MEASURES CRANBERRY JUICE

6 MEASURES SODA WATER

DRIED ORANGE WHEELS, TO GARNISH

Add the bourbon and marmalade to a jug and stir until dissolved.

Add all the remaining ingredients and fill the jug with ice cubes. Stir.

Garnish with dried orange wheels to serve.

JULEP PUNCH

6 MEASURES BOURBON

2 MEASURES LEMON JUICE

4 MEASURES SUGAR SYRUP

4 BLACK TEA BAGS

680 ML WATER

30 MINT LEAVES, PLUS EXTRA SPRIGS,

TO GARNISH

LEMON, TO GARNISH

Ahead of time, brew some strong black tea with 680 ml water and 4 teabags. Let it cool.

In a pitcher or bowl with ice, stir the cooled tea with the bourbon, lemon juice and sugar syrup.

Take 30 clean mint leaves and squeeze to release their essential oils. Add them to the punch and stir.

Garnish each glass with more mint sprigs and lemon wheels.

ATLANTIC CITY PUNCH

12 MEASURES SCOTCH WHISKY

2 MEASURES CINNAMON-INFUSED HONEY SYRUP

(SEE PAGE 115)

6 DASHES CHOCOLATE BITTERS

6 MEASURES SPARKLING WINE

CINNAMON STICK, TO GARNISH

In a pitcher or bowl with ice, combine the Scotch whisky, cinnamon-infused honey syrup and chocolate bitters.

Stir well, then fill with the sparkling wine.

Garnish with a cinnamon stick in each glass.

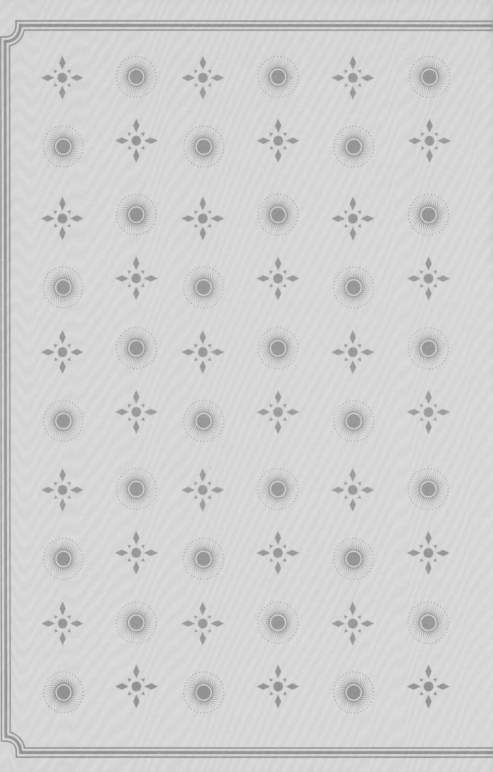

CLASSICS

OLD FASHIONED

2 MEASURES BOURBON

1 TSP SUGAR SYRUP

1 DASH ORANGE BITTERS

1 DASH ANGOSTURA BITTERS

ORANGE, TO GARNISH

Half-fill a glass with ice cubes.
Add the remaining ingredients to
the glass and stir for 1 minute.

Fill the glass with more ice cubes
and garnish with an orange twist.

PENICILLIN

2 MEASURES SCOTCH WHISKY

2 TSP ISLAY WHISKY

2 TSP GINGER JUICE

1 MEASURE SUGAR SYRUP

1 MEASURE LEMON JUICE

LEMON, TO GARNISH

Add all the ingredients to a cocktail shaker full of ice cubes.

Shake and strain into an old-fashioned glass filled with ice cubes.

Garnish with a lemon wedge.

RICKEY

1½ MEASURES BOURBON

1½ MEASURES LIME JUICE

SODA WATER, TO TOP

LIME, TO GARNISH

Put some ice cubes into a tall glass
with the bourbon and lime juice.

Top up with soda water and stir.

Garnish with a lime rind twist.

WHISKY
SOUR

2 MEASURES SCOTCH WHISKY

1 MEASURE LEMON JUICE

1 MEASURE SUGAR SYRUP

LEMON, TO GARNISH

Fill a cocktail shaker with ice cubes.

Add all the ingredients and shake.

Strain into a glass filled with ice cubes and garnish with a lemon wedge and a lemon rind spiral.

ROB ROY

1 MEASURE SCOTCH WHISKY

½ MEASURE VERMOUTH

1 DASH ANGOSTURA BITTERS

LEMON, TO GARNISH

Put a cracked ice cube, whisky, vermouth and bitters into a mixing glass and stir well.

Strain into a cocktail glass and garnish the rim with a lemon rind spiral.

RUSTY
NAIL

1½ MEASURES SCOTCH WHISKY

1 MEASURE DRAMBUIE

Fill an old-fashioned glass with ice cubes and pour the whisky and Drambuie over them.

Stir gently.

MANHATTAN

1 MEASURE SWEET VERMOUTH

3 MEASURES RYE WHISKEY OR BOURBON

COCKTAIL CHERRY, TO GARNISH (OPTIONAL)

Put 4–5 ice cubes into a mixing glass.

Pour the vermouth and whiskey over
the ice.

Stir vigorously, then strain into a
chilled cocktail glass and drop in
a cocktail cherry, if you like.

GODFATHER

2 MEASURES J&B RARE SCOTCH WHISKY

1 MEASURE AMARETTO DI SARONNO LIQUEUR

Put some ice cubes into a
cocktail shaker with the whisky
and Amaretto di Saronno and
shake vigorously.

Strain into a small old-fashioned
glass filled with ice cubes.

ALGONQUIN

1 MEASURE PINEAPPLE JUICE

1 MEASURE DRY VERMOUTH

3 MEASURES BOURBON OR SCOTCH WHISKY

Put some ice cubes into a mixing glass.

Pour the pineapple juice, vermouth and bourbon or whisky over the ice.

Stir vigorously until nearly frothy, then strain into a chilled cocktail glass.

Serve with a straw.

105

WHISKY MAC

1 MEASURE SCOTCH WHISKY

1 MEASURE GINGER WINE

Put the ice cubes into an old-fashioned glass.

Pour the whisky and ginger wine over the ice and stir slightly.

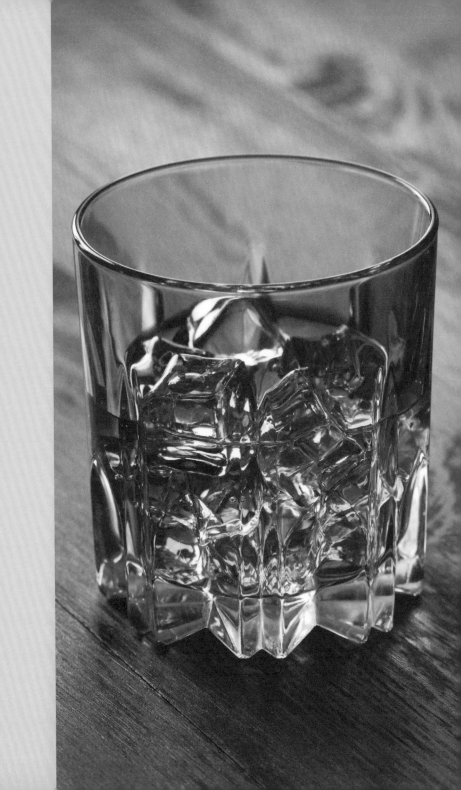

IRISH COFFEE

1½ MEASURES IRISH WHISKEY

½ MEASURE COFFEE LIQUEUR

1 MEASURE VANILLA SYRUP

2 MEASURES ESPRESSO

WHIPPED CREAM, TO TOP

Add all the ingredients, except the cream, to a small saucepan and gently heat till warm, but not boiling.

Pour into a rocks glass and top with whipped cream.

SAZERAC

2 ½ MEASURES RYE WHISKEY

2 DASHES PEYCHAUD'S BITTERS

1 DASH ANGOSTURA BITTERS

1 DASH ABSINTHE

1 SUGAR CUBE

1 DASH WATER

LEMON, TO GARNISH

Chill an old-fashioned glass or small tumbler in your freezer.

In a mixing glass, combine the sugar cube, Peychaud's Bitters, and a few drops of water. Mix until sugar is dissolved and add the whiskey. Add plenty of ice, and stir for another 30 seconds.

Pour the absinthe into your chilled glass, and rotate glass until the inside is well coated; discard the excess.

Strain the liquid from your mixing glass into the serving glass and twist a piece of lemon peel over the drink, to garnish.

MINT JULEP I

2 MEASURES BOURBON

4 DASHES ANGOSTURA BITTERS

1 TSP SUGAR SYRUP

10 MINT LEAVES, PLUS AN EXTRA SPRIG, TO GARNISH

Muddle the mint leaves, sugar syrup and bitters in a highball glass.

Fill the glass with crushed ice, then add the bourbon.

Stir well and garnish with a mint sprig.

Serve with a long straw.

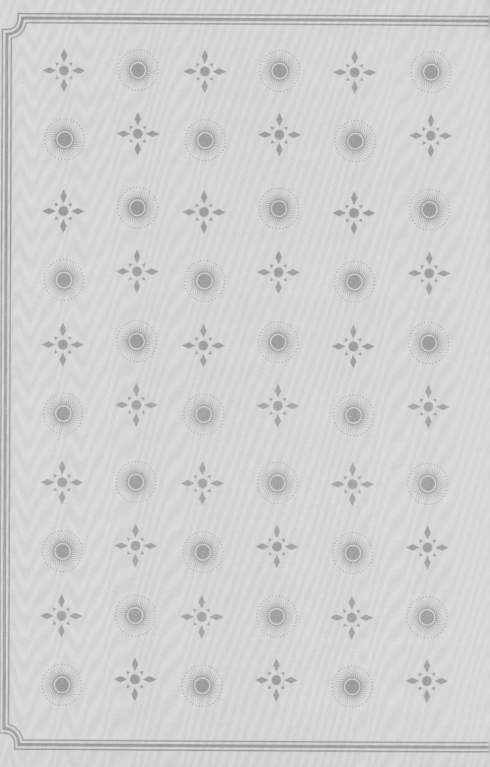

TIPS & TECHNIQUES FOR CRAFTING THE PERFECT COCKTAIL

WHAT MAKES A GOOD COCKTAIL?

Good cocktails, like good food, are based around quality ingredients. As with cooking, using fresh and homemade ingredients can often make the huge difference between a good drink and an outstanding drink. All of this can be found in department stores, online or in kitchen shops.

COCKTAIL INGREDIENTS

ICE This is a key part of cocktails and you'll need lots of it. Purchase it from your supermarket or freeze big tubs of water, then crack this up to use in your drinks. If you're hosting a big party and want to serve some punches, which will need lots of ice, it may be worthwhile finding if you have a local ice supplier that supplies catering companies, as this can be much more cost effective.

CITRUS JUICE It's important to use fresh citrus juice in your drinks; bottled versions taste awful and will not produce good drinks. Store your fruit out of the refrigerator at room temperature. Look for a soft-skinned fruit for juicing, which you can do with a juicer or citrus press. You can keep fresh citrus juice for a couple of days in the refrigerator, sealed to prevent oxidation.

SUGAR SYRUP You can buy sugar syrup or you can make your own. The most basic form of sugar syrup is made by mixing caster sugar and hot water together, and stirring until the sugar has dissolved. The key when preparing sugar syrups is to use a 1:1 ratio of sugar to liquid. White sugar acts as a flavour enhancer, while dark sugars have unique, more toffee flavours and work well with dark spirits.

BASIC SUGAR SYRUP RECIPE
(Makes 1 litre (1¾ pints) of sugar syrup)
Dissolve 1 kg (2 lb) caster sugar in 1 litre (1¾ pints) of hot water.
Allow to cool.
Sugar syrup will keep in a sterilized bottle stored in the refrigerator for up to 2 weeks.

ORANGE & CHERRY-INFUSED BOURBON
Muddle 6 slices orange and 6 glacier cherries in a jar and add 500 ml bourbon. Steep for 24 hours before straining. Follow same method for lemon or orange-infused bourbon.

CINNAMON-INFUSED HONEY SYRUP
In a saucepan over low heat, combine equal parts honey and water, stirring until the honey is dissolved. Add a cinnamon stick and let it steep for 20 to 30 minutes. Remove the cinnamon stick before use.

CHOOSING GLASSWARE

There are many different cocktails, but they all fall into one of three categories: long, short or shot. Long drinks generally have more mixer than alcohol, often served with ice and a straw. The terms 'straight up' and 'on the rocks' are synonymous with the short drink, which tends to be more about the spirit, often combined with a single mixer at most. Finally, there is the shot which is made up mainly from spirits and liqueurs, designed to give a quick hit of alcohol. Glasses are tailored to the type of drinks they will contain.

CHAMPAGNE FLUTE   Used for Champagne or Champagne cocktails, the narrow mouth of the flute helps the drink to stay fizzy.

CHAMPAGNE SAUCER   A classic glass, but not very practical for serving Champagne as the drink quickly loses its fizz.

MARGARITA OR COUPETTE GLASS   When used for a Margarita, the rim is dipped in salt. Also used for daiquiris and other fruit-based cocktails.

HIGHBALL GLASS   Suitable for any long cocktail, such as a Long Island Iced Tea.

COLLINS GLASS This is similar to a highball glass but is slightly narrower.

WINE GLASS Sangria is often served in one, but they are not usually used for cocktails.

OLD-FASHIONED GLASS Also known as a rocks glass, this is great for any drink that's served on the rocks or straight up.

SHOT GLASS Often found in two sizes — for a single or double measure. They are ideal for a single mouthful.

BALLOON GLASS Often used for fine spirits. The glass can be warmed to encourage the release of the drink's aroma.

HURRICANE GLASS Mostly found in beach bars, used for creamy, rum-based drinks.

BOSTON GLASS Often used by bartenders for mixing cocktails, good for fruity drinks.

TODDY GLASS A toddy glass is generally used for a hot drink, such as Irish Coffee.

SLING GLASS This has a very short stemmed base and is most famously used for a Singapore Sling.

MARTINI GLASS Also known as a cocktail glass, its thin neck design makes sure your hand can't warm the glass, or the cocktail.

USEFUL EQUIPMENT

Some pieces of equipment, such as shakers and the correct glasses, are vital for any cocktail party, while others, like ice buckets, can be obtained at a later date if needed. Below is a wishlist for anyone who wants to make cocktails on a regular basis.

SHAKER The Boston shaker is the most simple option, but it needs to be used in conjunction with a hawthorne strainer. Alternatively you could choose a shaker with a built-in strainer.

MEASURE OR JIGGER Single and double measures are available and are essential when you are mixing ingredients so that the proportions are always the same. One measure is 25 ml or 1 fl oz.

MIXING GLASS A mixing glass is used for those drinks that require only a gentle stirring before they are poured or strained.

HAWTHORNE STRAINER This type of strainer is often used in conjunction with a Boston shaker, but a simple tea strainer will also work well.

BAR SPOON Similar to a teaspoon but with a long handle, a bar spoon is used for stirring, layering and muddling drinks.

MUDDLING STICK Similar to a pestle, which will work just as well, a muddling stick, or muddler, is used to crush fruit or herbs in a glass or shaker for drinks like the Mojito.

BOTTLE OPENER Choose a bottle opener with two attachments, one for metal-topped bottles and a corkscrew for wine bottles.

POURERS A pourer is inserted into the top of a spirit bottle to enable the spirit to flow in a controlled manner.

FOOD PROCESSOR A food processor or blender is useful for making frozen cocktails and smoothies.

EQUIPMENT FOR GARNISHING Many drinks are garnished with fruit on cocktail sticks and these are available in wood, plastic or glass. Exotic drinks may be prettified with a paper umbrella and several long drinks are served with straws or swizzle sticks.

TECHNIQUES

With just a few basic techniques, your bartending skills will be complete. Follow the instructions to hone your craft.

BLENDING Frozen cocktails and smoothies are blended with ice in a blender until they are of a smooth consistency. Be careful not to add too much ice as this will dilute the cocktail. It's best to add a little at a time.

SHAKING The best-known cocktail technique and probably the most common. Used to mix ingredients thoroughly and quickly, and to chill the drink before serving.
1 Half-fill a cocktail shaker with ice cubes, or cracked or crushed ice.
2 If the recipe calls for a chilled glass add a few ice cubes and some cold water to the glass, swirl it around and discard.
3 Add the ingredients to the shaker and shake until a frost forms on the outside.
4 Strain the cocktail into the glass and serve.

MUDDLING A technique used to bring out the flavours of herbs and fruit using a blunt tool called a muddler.
1 Add chosen herb(s) to a highball glass. Add some sugar syrup and some lime wedges.
2 Hold the glass firmly and use a muddler or pestle to twist and press down.

3 Continue for 30 seconds, top up with crushed ice and add remaining ingredients.

DOUBLE-STRAINING   To prevent all traces of puréed fruit and ice fragments from entering the glass, use a shaker with a built-in strainer in conjunction with a hawthorne strainer. A fine strainer also works well.

LAYERING   Some spirits can be served layered on top of each other, causing 'lighter' spirits to float on top of your cocktail.
1 Pour the first ingredient into a glass, taking care that it does not touch the sides.
2 Position a bar spoon in the centre of the glass, rounded part down and facing you. Rest the spoon against the side of the glass as your pour the second ingredient down the spoon. It should float on top of the first liquid.
3 Repeat with the third ingredient, then carefully remove the spoon.

STIRRING   Used when the ingredients need to be mixed and chilled, but also maintain their clarity. This ensures there are no ice fragments or air bubbles throughout the drink. Some cocktails require the ingredients to be prepared in a mixing glass, then strained into the serving glass.
1 Add ingredients to a glass, in recipe order.
2 Use a bar spoon to stir the drink, lightly or vigorously, as described in the recipe.
3 Finish the drink with any decoration and serve.

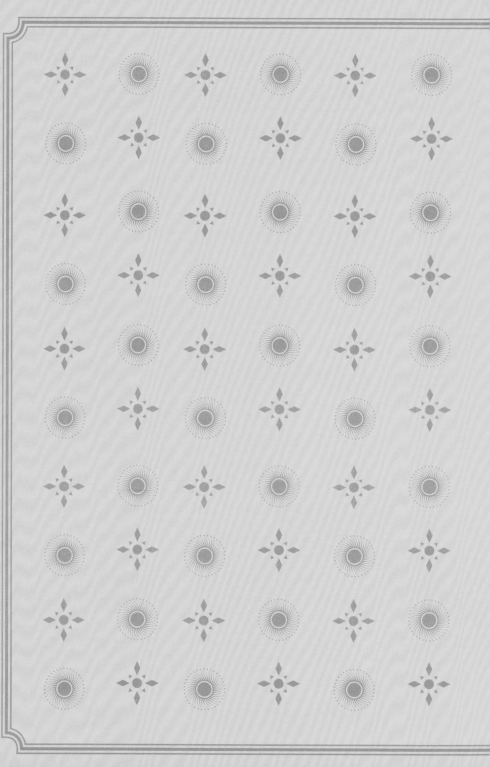

INDEX

127

128

PICTURE CREDITS

123RF Boris Ryzhkov 40; Brent Hofacker 16, 21; Charles Wollertz 110; fesenko 52; Volodymyr Krasyuk 107. **Dreamstime** Bhofack2 102. **Octopus Publishing Group** Jonathan Kennedy 13, 25, 28, 33, 59, 64, 84, 89, 94, 99; Stephen Conroy 37, 47, 71, 7; William Reavell 81.